Perfect PENGUINS

ADÉLIE PENGUIN

Written by Bethany Latham

Enslow PUBLISHING

Published in 2026 by Enslow Publishing, LLC
2544 Clinton Street
Buffalo, NY 14224

Written by: Bethany Latham
Edited by: Rebecca Phillips-Bartlett
Designed by: Amy Li

Cataloging-in-Publication Data

Names: Latham, Bethany, author.
Title: Adélie penguin / Bethany Latham.
Description: Buffalo, NY : Enslow Publishing, 2026. | Series: Perfect penguins | Includes glossary and index.
Identifiers: ISBN 9781978547346 (pbk.) | ISBN 9781978547353 (library bound) | ISBN 9781978547360 (ebook)
Subjects: LCSH: Adélie penguin--Juvenile literature.
Classification: LCC QL696.S473 L834 2026 | DDC 598.47--dc23

Manufactured in the United States of America

CPSIA compliance information: Batch #QW26ENS: For further information contact Enslow Publishing LLC, New York, New York at 1-800-398-2504.

IMAGE CREDITS

All images are courtesy of Shutterstock.com, unless otherwise stated.

Recurring – Martyshova Maria (doodles and arrows). Cover – Agami Photo Agency, pixuberant. 2–3 – Mozgova. 4–5 – Danita Delimont, Alfie Photography, Traveller MG, Dr_Flash. 6–7 – iDef Images, cnicolestudio, Nick Dale Photo. 8–9 – Mariusz Potocki, Sandra Ophorst, LouieLea. 10–11 – NaturesMomentsuk, Armin Rose. 12–13 – Mozgova, Alexey Seafarer. 14–15 – demamiel62. 16–17 – Danita Delimont, Harald Lang. 18–19 – Tarpan, Subphoto.com, Ztutte. 20–21 – Kaspars Grinvalds, Risto Raunio. 22–23 – Steve Allen, pixuberant.

CONTENTS

WORDS THAT LOOK LIKE THIS CAN BE FOUND IN THE GLOSSARY ON PAGE 24.

ADÉLIE PENGUINS

Unlike most birds, penguins cannot fly. Instead, their flippers are used to help them swim. There are 18 species of penguins living in many different places in the world.

ROCKHOPPER PENGUIN

GALAPAGOS PENGUIN

EMPEROR PENGUIN

Adélie penguins are medium-sized penguins. They grow to be around 2.3 feet (70 cm) tall. Adélie penguins were discovered in the 1800s by a French explorer. He named the penguins after his wife, Adèle.

HABITAT

Adélie penguins live in Antarctica. Antarctica is one of the coldest places in the world. Five types of penguins live in Antarctica, including Adélies. Adélie penguins are found in many different parts of Antarctica.

An animal's natural home is called its habitat.

In summer, Adélie penguins live on and around Antarctica's islands and rocky coast. They lay their eggs in rocky places. In the winter, the penguins travel to the ice and sea to hunt.

BODY

Adélie penguins have orange-colored beaks. Their beaks are half covered with feathers, which makes them look shorter than they are. Adélie penguins have pink feet with strong black claws. Their claws are good for climbing.

Adélie penguins have long feathers on the backs of their heads. They can lift these feathers to make a crest. Adélie penguin feathers are usually waterproof. Once a year, they shed their waterproof feathers.

Adults have a ring of white feathers around their eyes.

GETTING AROUND

Adélie penguins are great swimmers and divers. They can swim much faster than they can walk. Adélie penguins can dive down to 575 feet (175 m). They can hold their breath underwater for up to six minutes.

While they are swimming, Adélie penguins often jump in and out of the water. This is called porpoising. Scientists think the penguins do this so they can move faster and confuse predators.

ADÉLIE PENGUINS PORPOISING

LIFE CYCLE

A life cycle is the stages of an animal's life that lead to the animal having their own young.

Adélie penguins mate in the Antarctic spring. Adélie penguins sing and wave their heads to find a mate. Many penguins have one mate that they return to each year.

The father builds a nest out of rocks. Around November, the mother lays two eggs in the nest. The mother and father take turns looking after the eggs.

The eggs hatch in December after about six weeks. Adélie penguin chicks are gray or black and very fluffy. They do not have white feathers around their eyes yet. Instead, the feathers are black.

Chicks huddle together for safety in groups called crèches. Adélie chicks start hunting by themselves at around nine weeks old. They can have their own young after they are three years old.

Adélie penguins live 11 to 20 years in the wild.

FAMILY LIFE

Adélie penguins are very social animals. Many thousands come to the rocky beaches to mate and lay eggs. Each male tries to build a bigger nest than the others. Sometimes, they steal rocks from other nests.

Adélie penguins are very curious and feisty. They will defend themselves from predators by flapping at them and hitting them with their flippers. Sometimes, they will even hit scientists.

DIET AND DANGERS

Adélie penguins eat a lot of krill. They also eat Antarctic silverfish. When they are hunting in the ocean, the penguins stay near the surface where they can see better.

A diet is the type of food an animal eats.

Adélie penguins are in danger of being eaten by orcas and leopard seals. These animals hunt the penguins when they are swimming in the ocean. Leopard seals also hunt Adélie penguins through thin ice.

PROTECT THE PENGUINS

Scientists do not think Adélie penguins are in danger of dying out soon. Adélie penguin numbers are growing in some parts of Antarctica. However, they are still at risk from climate change.

Melting ice in some parts of Antarctica means there are fewer Adélie penguins in those areas. Scientists are studying the penguins to see where they are traveling and how they are affected by climate change.

PERFECT PENGUINS

Adélie penguins are small but mighty birds. We have seen that they are feisty and curious animals. What are some words you would use to describe your personality?

Scientists think Adélies are a perfect penguin to study. What type of wildlife would you like to study?

What was your favorite Adélie penguin fact? Do you think you would like to meet an Adélie penguin?

GLOSSARY

CLIMATE CHANGE	a change in the typical weather or temperature of a large area
COAST	where the land meets the sea
CREST	a section of feathers, fur, or skin on the top of an animal's head
FEISTY	brave and tough, with lots of energy
MATE	to produce young with an animal of the same species
PREDATORS	animals that hunt other animals for food
SHED	to remove and replace part of the body, such as the skin or a shell, with another one that has grown underneath
SOCIAL	to do with being in a group or community
SPECIES	a group of very similar animals or plants that can create young together
SURFACE	the top layer of a body of water

INDEX